MY FIRST
30 FRUITS

Kids Coloring Book

THICK AND BOLD LINES

NINA LARS

This Book Belongs To

BANANA

APPLE

MANGO

STRAWBERRY

GUAVA

NECTARINE

KIWI

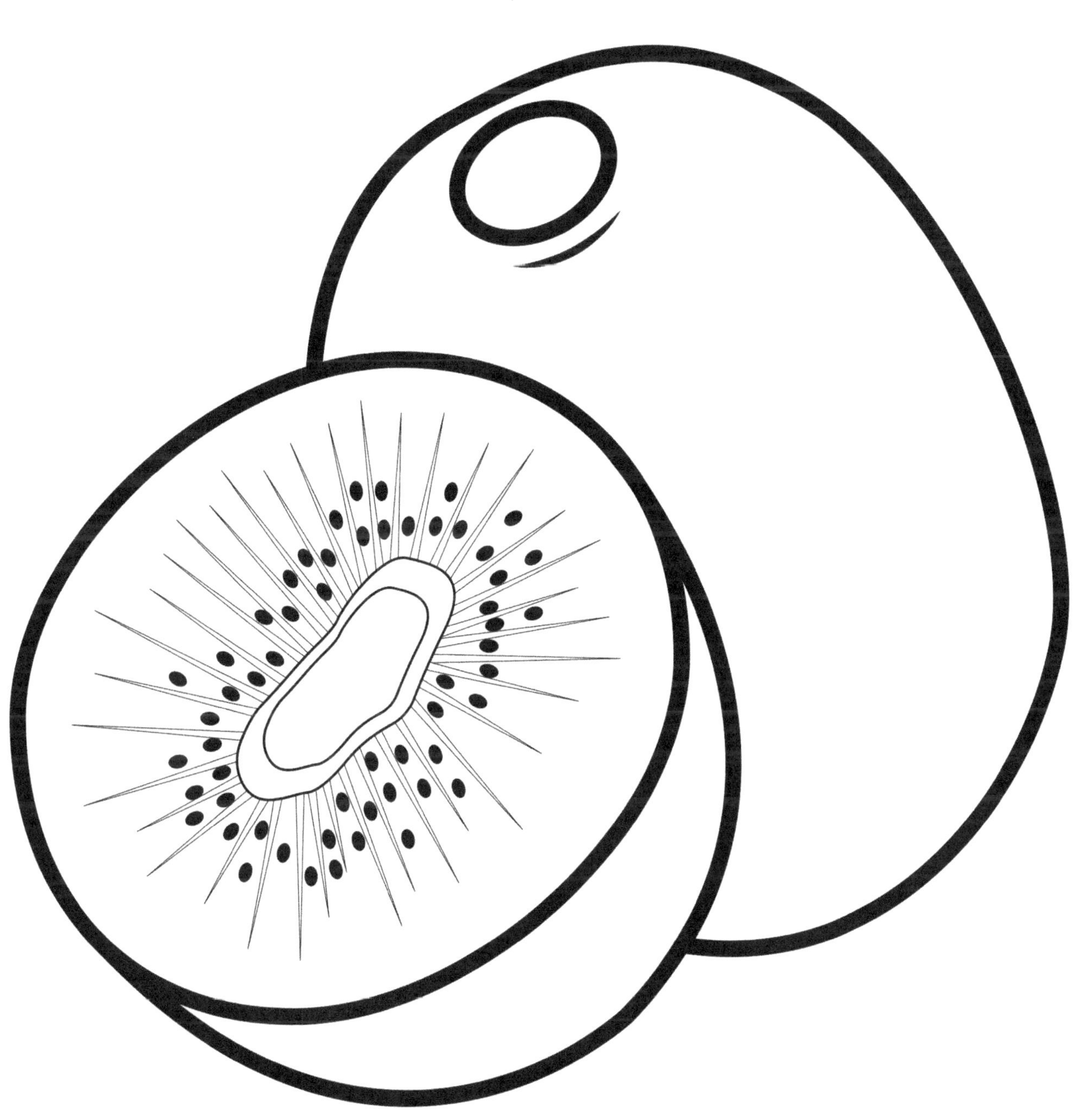

COCONUT

SNAKE FRUIT

DRAGON FRUIT

PEACH

ORANGE

DATE-PLUM

DURIAN

PINEAPPLE

CHERRY

AVOCADO

WATERMELON

GRAPES

PAPAYA

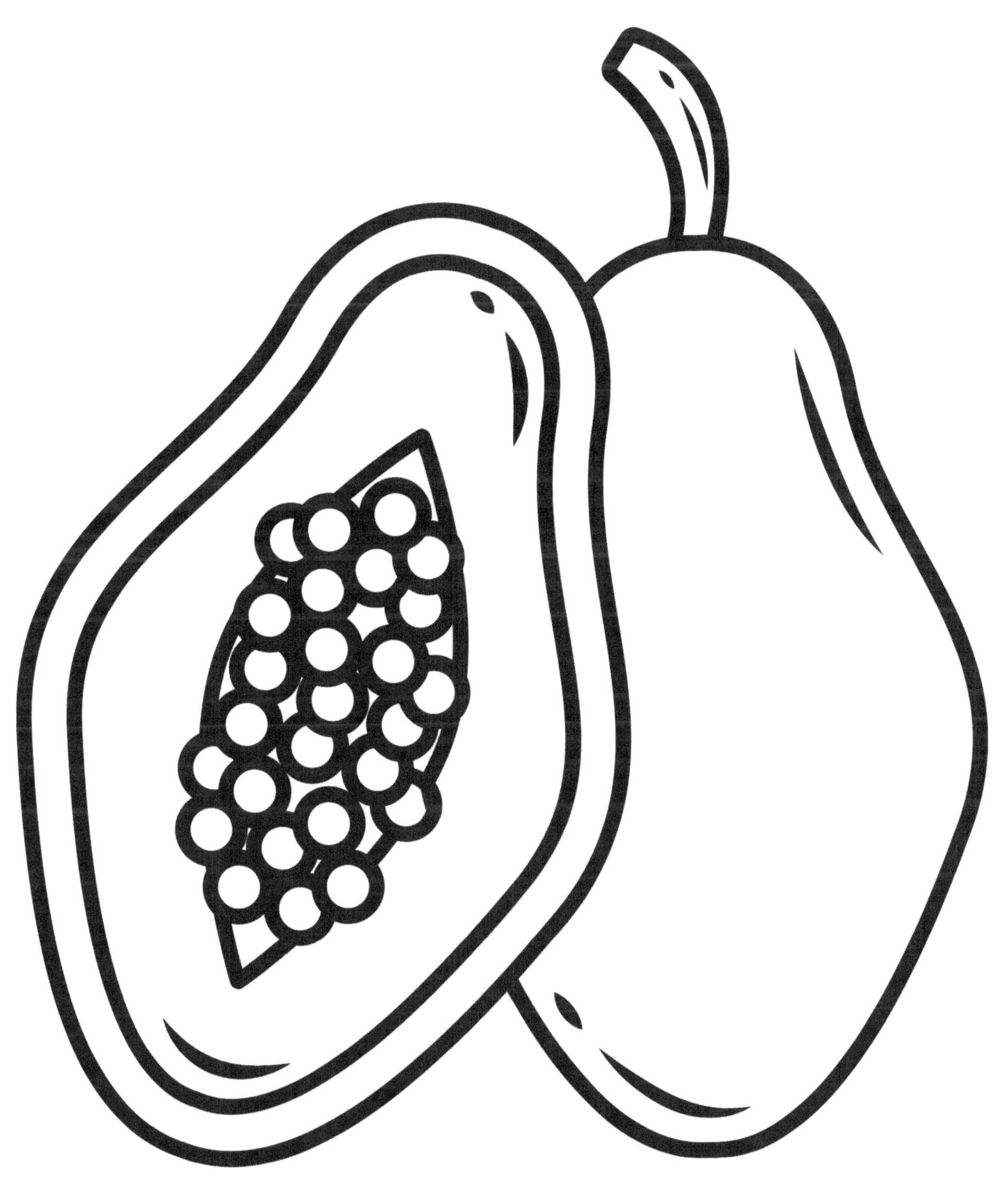

STAR FRUIT

MELON

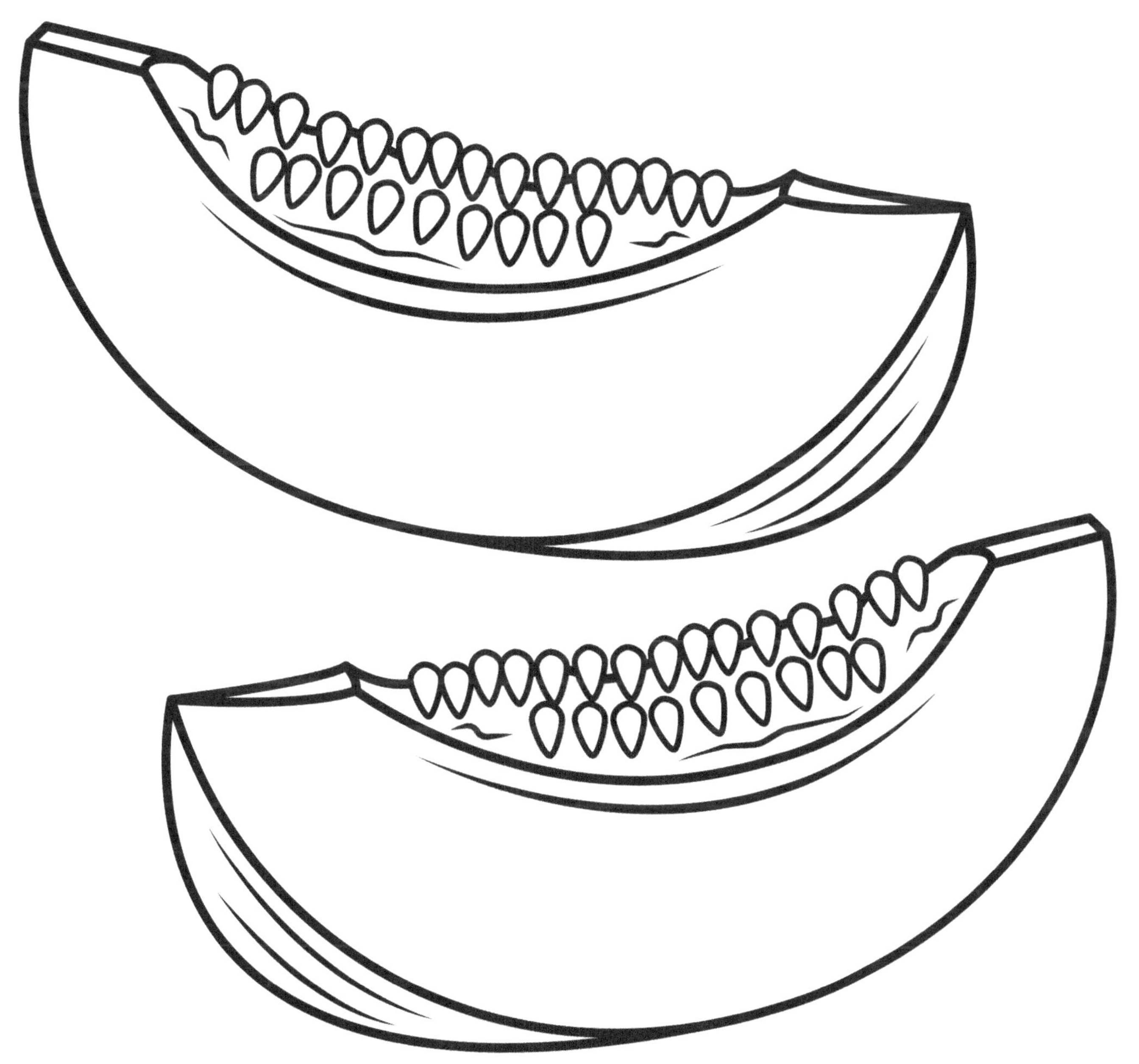

LEMON

POMEGRANATE

MANGOSTEEN

APRICOT

QUINCE

KUMQUAT

GOOSEBERRY

LOQUAT